George Kalamaras

That Moment of Wept

ŜV

SurVision Books

First published in 2018 by
SurVision Books
Dublin, Ireland
www.survisionmagazine.com

Cover image: Detail from a painting by Paul Klee, "Little Hope," 1938, from the Berggruen Klee Collection, 1984 (the Metropolitan Museum of Art)

Author photo by Jim Whitcraft

ISBN: 978-1-9995903-7-6

for Mary Ann and Bootsie—always

and for the belovèd yogis of India

Other Books by George Kalamaras

POETRY

The Hermit's Way of Being Human (2015)

The Mining Camps of the Mouth (2012)

Kingdom of Throat-Stuck Luck (2011)

Symposium on the Body's Left Side (2011)

Your Own Ox-Head Mask as Proof (2010)

The Recumbent Galaxy (2010)
(with Alvaro Cardona-Hine)

Something Beautiful Is Always Wearing the Trees (2009)
(with paintings by Alvaro Cardona-Hine)

The Scathering Sound (2009)

Gold Carp Jack Fruit Mirrors (2008)

Even the Java Sparrows Call Your Hair (2004)

Borders My Bent Toward (2003)

The Theory and Function of Mangoes (2000)

Beneath the Breath (1988)

Heart Without End (1986)

CRITICISM

*Reclaiming the Tacit Dimension: Symbolic Form
in the Rhetoric of Silence* (1994)

Acknowledgments

I want to thank the editors of the following magazines in which nearly all of these poems, or their previous versions, first appeared:

Aldebaran Review: "If Not Perfect"

The Bitter Oleander: "The Practice of Gray Rain," "Because I Am a Pleasant Reason," "You Keep Telling Me," "The Give Give Grief," "The Methodology of Rain," "Parsing of the Bowels," "The Journey Inward (Body Time No More)," and "River Crossing"

Black Tongue Review: "Proof of the Theorem of Rising Hills"

Calibanonline: "The Healing Seam," "Archaeology," "Something Private and Sly," "There Are Many Beards in the Way One Sleeps," "Trying to Track Down Your Least-Open, Your Cracking-Closed, Heart," "Everything I Have Ever Sad Somehow Says Through You," "Ravens Dirging My Chest," "The Cause and Effect of Multiple Births," "The Texture of Milk," "If We Could Practice Each Other, We'd Be the World," "Almost Imaginable," and "Curious"

Dispatches from the Poetry Wars: "More Than a Noun," "Sphragistics," "Nothing Is Ever as Clearly Written as the Owl's Insomnia," "Sad Enough for Seventeen-and-a-Half Incarnations," "Breathing Us Broken," "A Hundred-Year Conversation," "The Agony of Compassion," "Colorblind," "Invasive Species," "The Momentary Anguish of Repair," "The Powerful Dissolve of a Monk," "You're Afraid of a Dead Echo?" "Critical Dispersal," "Sorry," "In All My Blindness," "If I Were the Direction West," "The Exact Cost of Fish," "Reversing the Gaze," "African Sleep Sickness," and "The Sacred and the Profane"

International Gallerie: A Journal of Ideas (Mumbai, India): "Two Women Whose Clear Heads Cut Clear Through to Sad"

SurVision: "The Friction of Your Speak," "There Is Never Any Need to Cry," "Of Course," "A Pattern of Dexterity," and "That Moment of Wept"

Talisman: "Will You Not Kiss Me?" "Cut," "Each of Seven Months," "The One I Named," "Border of Yes, Contusion of No," and "Well Short"

Wilderness House Literary Review: "The Air Was Always Beautiful"

X-Peri: "I Don't Know Anything Anymore," "The Great Defecator," "The Incubation of *This* and *That*," "Extravagant Slaughter," and "The Sad Textile of Your Eye"

I would like to thank my wife, Mary Ann Cain, for her unending inspiration and support, as we share our lives, work, and love. I'm also immensely grateful to John Bradley for his thoughtful and generous commentary on my poems, none of which would be the same without all we share. Huge thanks, as well, goes to Eric Baus, Ray Gonzalez, Patrick Lawler, John Olson, Paul B. Roth, Tony Trigilio, and Lawrence R. Smith. No acknowledgment would be complete, however, without honoring the life and teachings of Paramahansa Yogananda.

CONTENTS

The Friction of Your Speak

The Agony of Compassion

The Deliberate Dead of Continuously Laying Ourselves Bare

Everything I Have Ever Sad Somehow Says Through You

Mud Cells of Excellent Milk

"The books are friendly but have terrible minds of their own."
—George Stanley

"The air is a beautiful princess without bones."
—Takiguchi Shūzō

The Friction of Your Speak

The Air Was Always Beautiful

Then I emerged, briefly, as a centipede.
I had carried over the karma of math and needed to learn to count
    on myself for everything.

That's not a joke.
Forgive me if I believed I'd never live past one hundred.

Then I was human again, this time a childhood chess master from
    Peru.
I remember grieving the copper miners whose veins corroded like
    neglected knob and tube, who coughed as if they were in love
    with death.

This was a long time ago.
There were decades of black and red, knights flanking bishops,
    bishops gripping their groin, wanting to jump the queen.

The air was always beautiful.
I kept a bird in my chest and periodically asked it to teach me how
    to swim.

Now the carpet cleaners have come, bringing me a formula for dust
    mites.
They seem baffled when I say, *I would never kill another living
    thing.*

The Friction of Your Speak

Caught by a line of depth, we fought the mighty word of our bodies.
You asked if my name in French meant *sophisticated carnivore*.

I must confess—I rarely eat apples.
I am reminded of the garden and how my nakedness feels both
    ways at once.

Harness in the thought, as you might consider an obscure baseball
    statistic to prevent the premature release of your breath's
    breath.
I'm here to tell you it doesn't work—that my thoughts scatter like
    tiny burrows of lice larvae into the friction of your speak.

My life appeared to be a sum cosmetically equal to 1.56 British
    pounds, thirty-three Indian rupees, and sixty million years of
    Tasmanian salt.
If you called me a specimen, I'd interrogate your food.

A piece of work? You consider me something *made*, difficult to
    reach?
There is a mole track beneath my word, passing into darkness
    without my feet. When you lowered your lip onto mine, it was
    revealed.

Say the Craving Whole

Is it sorrow I seek or the sad of your mouth?
We touch tongues as if enacting sacred talk.

Once, when I had a body, I was throbbing inside your thighs, alive.
Then I awoke on a plain of emu skulls and realized my birth.

The great goose gave me grave advice.
Calendar after calendar I'd only wanted more.

I have been traveling a long mouth from now.
Trembling in the sexual act, I have tried to and stutter-blood and
    speech.

Each of the spinal centers is alive with quieted craving.
Which will I seek as I round myself to now?

If you want to know me, know yourself as more than what you hide.
Human skin. Worm-ridden urge. Floss against our speech.

I am that, more or less, as I inhabit this skin momentary years
    descended from that star.
I am about to be birthed into monk-mouth, monkfish, or more, and
    to say the craving whole.

More Than a Noun

I am amazed at the pain of a word and how it releases me.
Land of contemplative frock coats, do not lend me your blame.

Sweet weeping from the intestinal tunnel of a crow.
I must pass through with the entire congregation of half-eaten
hyacinths.

Dentist or ornithologist?
Ophthalmologist or soothsayer?

I require a pharyngeal exam but do not know whose urge to insert
first.
Hers or mine? Both of our predictions are tenuous.

To that virtue of loneliness, I might add the raucous cough of a
three a.m. train.
To the late-at-night departing dimple, I might add a remembrance
of Swiss cheese, of apple and salt, of how now your mouth.

I could love your bee entrail if you would remove it from your chest
and set it ablaze—in my mouth—with the sand fleas you seek.
Hair framing your face, making you more than a feminine ending,
you are here, noun-wise, holding forth a bottle of burned
eyelashes you retrieved—over many months of sleep—from the
stomach of the underground bear.

There Is Never Any Need to Cry

There is never any need to cry for me.
Cry for the tea leaves, poured onto the napkin, in the shape of the
  Milky Way.

We transform a grumble into a gunwale.
We mark our mouths with lime.

Time passes like a grasshopper's wings.
We know the rhythm of what we *should* know yet still examine our
  groins with strange fascination.

Did you find the terrestrial mountain shrimp inside the music of
  possible rain?
Might the hermit crabs scuttling in their nocturnal crate offer a
  psychic weight that is somehow lighter than despair?

When you arrive, send me a postcard from a different port.
Carry it first, so that it contains a postmark from the next town
  over.

There are mutual galaxies vast as the rainy season in a rain-soaked
  sleeve.
That's why when it rains I feel finally whole.

The Practice of Gray Rain

Don't you admit the iridescence of dead sheep into the kingdom of
    rainwater?
Can't you crawl the flock's bawling back across the field as if struck
    dumb by darkness?

As if all the umbrellas in the world suddenly opened into swans.
As if we passed the sleepwalking fluid mouth to mouth like a great
    woolen mood.

Don't kiss me, please, if you require us both to be safe.
Fashion me a way to live with animals, to say my name with
    unconditional madness.

I have sinned far too often in the right hand of the many-toed.
I have come of it and exacerbated the melancholy of too much
    private profusion.

The unbreakable hymen of desire hisses a fabulous sweat.
I know. I have removed the letters *B* and *S*, *O* and *K*, from my
    vocabulary of sheared lambs and meaningful sensual response.

It is difficult, they say, to hear one's own release as it transmutes
    into internal rain.
I had been a Taoist mountain-recluse and had practiced invigorating
    starlight from mud, but was reborn a primitive nerve impulse, an
    electrical storm of a most gray rain.

Will You Not Kiss Me?

After mastering the breath, we come to know every birth, each in
	proper order.
The deserts of Tartary in 1844 are an escorted situation.

It is said that Prince Shōtoku created this Buddhist nunnery in
	600 C.E.
But this is the unreliable history, more like a wall of cross-legged
	images partially smeared with candle soot and incense.

Trying to ask my face the weight of two crows confuses the mirror.
I hold up two fingers and fear the butcher, even his russet
	mushroom.

Will you not kiss me and abruptly advance my requiem?
The breathing nucellus shepherds a jackal into and out of my open
	chest.

A most unexpected breath may occident my raincoat.
It might compass-mouth my ear, with or without your maritime
	tongue.

At the end of the sea-lesions, I found a remarkable intimacy.
After months afloat, I was still craving your breath against my chest.
	My mouth moved on demand, and I never knew the darkness
	of your blind voluptuous eclipse.

The Healing Seam

There is a colorful dream experiment, and I am it.
We can dark-logic our shape, but we end up empty.

Spill the plaid of your shadow-leaf hand.
Let me open my own and breathe the bloated soul.

Seal hole over which, harpoon-ready, I hang?
Something like cold in my bone when I relinquish logical thought to
    the snow cave I crave?

I have been smelling too many windy pines.
I have been stalking the canebrake, my furry dream-shirt not yet
    silk.

These are the deaths to which I stink.
Smell our casual glance, slow-feed it to each other on the street, in
    a café, in a most susceptible embrace, blur by blur, awaiting
    the healing seam of the dream.

Because I Am a Pleasant Reason

I inhabited the green flaking paint of a Paris park bench.
I had been on my way to Somalia to study a rare species of snail
blood.

Yes, blood can be a species. Because I am a pleasant reason, you
leave, guiding braids of escorted hair.
Look at the translation of your arm. Count the air syllables in my
mouth.

Bawdy seaside humor is a metaphor for fluctuating breath.
Support my chin with your wrist, and I will hold your gauze forever.

Look: the impulsive weave of late-night work leaves me craving an
illicit kerosene caress.
I would only kiss you if I was assured of the compliance of your
poison.

Renegotiate a sincere frustration on any African coast and require a
closer world.
There are more possibilities for tenderness than my mouth—slow-
crawling across dirt—could ever possibly extract.

You Keep Telling Me

Spread your malaria before me with all the display of a strutting
   peacock.
Let me hear your equatorial cohesions. Suture even those that are
   most firm.

Constant. You keep telling me about the boy I was and was not.
You want me to eat vegetables of the moon from the tin roof of an
   Indiana shed.

I invite you over, but—mysteriously—you're already here.
I ask you your name and repeat that it *is* my business.

Coffee. We sit together as if we both lacked a packet of sugar and
   swizzle stick.
The nerve-ridden brown circle on the ceiling suggests our ascending
   stain.

I wish I could explore your most secret vowel in my mouth.
I'm not talking just any old kiss but a sliding of enlivened bees like
   familial mirrors in the bloodlines.

Concern. You have at least some scar or other you'd like to impart?
You hold my hand, look deeply into my eye as if displacing a full
   glass of water with a cube. Tell me you're the one who's cold
   because I'm the one who's not.

Sphragistics

I studied the seal and signet of your mouth.
I considered kissing but then remembered my life.

It is strange how dropsy rarely occurs in the inguinal canal.
A diluted hawk moth is actually a riverous blood vessel?

She set the bird on fire and said Joseph Cornell should shave.
What business did he have exhuming the corpse of each tiny box?

It wasn't until last week that the palaver got to me.
Idle *this*. Charm and beguile *that*.

We count our stitches to ten and stop at what the mystics call *teth*.
What better way than to recite our scar back through a Sumerian
    alphabet.

The dropwort of Eurasia bears small white flowers.
We stuped the hamstring, studied our insignias, and relinquished
    every tetchy joy.

Nothing Is Ever as Clearly Written as the Owl's Insomnia

And so my referential. My just this side of yesterday. My owl mouth
and spit.
It has been written, *Goldfish in the brain equals the wanton blue
river of your wrist.*

And so my deconstructed. My please. My most and wanted and
salt.
It is said sideways at midnight into a possum's ear, *Which is your
left and which your right?—ear, I mean, not snout nor pouch nor
most deeply disturbed nocturnal beyond.*

In *Responses Magnetic*, Kijima Hajime traces the flute playing of an
old-forested owl.
In *Residence on Earth*, Neruda finds the terrestrial bone of a woven
blue afghan cannot keep him warm, cannot possibly keep *any of
us* warm.

And so my funerary oil that I avoid. My drowning number. My
bloodied *get-up-and-go* and wet sector of *yes* with blood-mulch
and bone.
And so my voice, dispersed as a shadow over an onion, a Bermuda
onion not yet purple in wounded rings of pursuit.

It has been written, somewhere inside me, *I could die if they'd but
let me.*
It has been written and written and written, perhaps by me or
through the midnight feather stir of an owl shivering off the
moist:

Here, take my tongue—repulsive fragment of a tempest—taste its
fierce owl-nest needles, its rivers and its transaction, its ever-
throbbing moan.
Take its woven blue bone blood-mapping this name of mine,
endlessly, to yours, to ours, to something our mouths cannot
possibly conceive.

Sad Enough for Seventeen-and-a-Half Incarnations

They say that when one plant in the room is cut, all the others
  psychically bleed.
I learned from the yogi not to eat in public so as not to ingest the
  asthma of others.

I've been lost and sad enough for at least seventeen-and-a-half
  incarnations.
It's time to rejoice in the broken fork, even in the unrelenting grasp
  of the napkin ring.

I figured I'd count backwards from sweater to vest to bare-skinned
  chest.
We arrive and grow with much expectation. As kids we think
  staying up past ten will one day salve every possible bleed.

I look around the room and solve many hosts.
They invite me in. To myself. Where I am rarely at rest.

You want to enter your blood in a contest against mine?
You're convinced that Douglas really bit off Lincoln's ear in the ring
  of the great debate? That Alexander unsheathed his sword into
  the bowels of a burning book?

Alright. I've had enough of trying to relive your parasite in the
  deaths of my lower folds.
I won't take my meal before you, but I will hold your head tenderly
  against my chest and wipe away—from us *both*—any tear you
  might give or sad or joyfully grieve.

The Agony of Compassion

Breathing Us Broken

Anyone can burn the kerosene rag and lie naked on a pile of
    pestiferous flies.
Diseases of breathing come in and out, out and in, breaking what
    we are.

In other economies, the long rib of dislocation is legal tender.
Here, eat this wolf. Bake this mud wasp into one part waste, two
    parts mouth.

Anyone can outlast the legend of the womb.
Bring a flower, a crack of crocodile dung from my ear, and bow
    before it.

The scar of its echo is called, *The Dual Breath Breathing Us Broken*.
In other discourses, we might pluck the snapdragon of death
    without returning to inhale significantly strutting crow blood.

Is the translation acceptable?
Will you swap saliva for kerosene, and either heat your home with
    reprise or die swallowing back what you've already broken?

I Don't Know Anything Anymore

So part of me was inflicting parallel wounds unto myself.
It was as if on a deck in the Atlantic I somehow whipped myself with
    cat-o'-nine-tails.

God, I loved her body, the rise and fall of her waves.
I imagine it's objectifying to both women and nature to eroticize
    the frenzied feedings of ants?

My body was covered in them, dream boils I was delighted to wake
    and forget.
I kept scratching death off my list as a possible freedom.

I was talking to Patrick about it, just Thursday.
He said, *Here, sneeze into this hanky the sad sad goldfish of your
    brain*, but he was hundreds of miles away and handing me
    nothing.

Nothing has prepared me for not knowing anything anymore.
My inside cry is a great good calm.

So I painted the green swan under Alvaro's tutelage.
But the swan wasn't green, only a certain shape of white.

This is how it comes, slow at first and then even slower, thick as
    gesso thinning.
Parallel wounds are rarely parallel only to themselves.

Were you confused last night when I entered your sleep?
You thought your fingers were alone until I touched you in your
    secret touching of me?

I have asked myself to spare me from this sudden inscription of
   pain.
Yes, I have borne many difficult deaths—some of myself and some
   of the sea, with its great green ways of sinking me.

Cut

Ambiguous hour of snow.
Ambage of blood lending oxygen one thought at a time.

The sound of dentures trying to speak, trapped in a glass.
Exaggerated underwater nouns when we talk to one another with a
     lamp.

All this. And frost and snow.
All this. And saltpeter in the belly of an elk.

How much of me has fallen, one haunch at a time?
Poor thing human language cannot possibly describe.

Frightful coat hanger in my room, doing everything the soul resists.
It hangs there, solitary, holding only the body of the day.

Prop of the hour, lean upon *me* for a change.
Each time I am reborn, the yogi said, *taking on a new body is like
     putting on an old overcoat.*

If a poisonous tango were to revoke my fever?
If a malarial yellow, if an Amazonian breast and how the missing
     one means strength?

If the photograph of a happy friendship dissolves?
If the doubtful river digs for cut, horizontal bones?

If the blue. The inevitable blue.
If the clear, evident blue.

Archaeology

I did not list the slightly bruised.
I would willingly transport the silence as a predator of thunder.

The dead second floor suite choked the best hotel air on a monthly
    basis.
I could break glass across the burial mounds of sugar west of the
    Wabash and create a new archaeology.

We appear to call one another by our Christian names.
I am known as *Dangling Austerity on My Side*. You, as *Take a Long
    Walk to Maximize Creative Capacity*.

We explored the hecatombs. We studied the Knights Templar.
We became Masons and cracked the universal cure for a private
    network of sickness.

Of course, I unzipped my pants when I peed in the public restroom.
I imagined you in the next room, between the walls of your stall,
    carefully measuring the month with a stained finger and
    trembling stained hand.

If Not Perfect

You said nothing about the stain on the cover of Vallejo's *Trilce*.
You hand me an ostrich feather as if I had never truly been alive, as
   if my savannah grass had only ever been ash.

We end up dying over a lunch of buttered bread.
I collide with my insides and finally get the joke.

But the table shakes as if the earth had a friend.
You and I have known one another's toe in a different shoe.

Walk like an animal and spoon me your source.
I could investigate finishing my life by walking—dumbly—room to
   room.

The way your singular kindness covers my infatuation with all things
   brassiere.
The sound of midnight trains has always been erotic in their long
   cat-crawl and dominating sleep.

A Hundred-Year Conversation

Apparently, the sad duty of the sea had something to do with
    music.
Not so long ago we could hear it as bee spica in the right ear.

How much of a hundred-year conversation had been eclipsed by a
    verbatim tuning of the brain?
We knew we were inmates of the body and accepted each written
    sentence as such.

One way to assure a wrong look is to require an expiration date on
    every lost chord.
We sniff milk and paw the dirt. We stiff-collar the smell. We require
    papers of infallible inquest.

So I'm afraid of an all-too-historical sleep?
Only animals humble their rapidly passing selves with unfledged
    loyalty to empty space?

Several rare and rangy hills mess with the aura of research.
My earliest expedition was the study of a commerce of collapsed
    hands reaching for an evaporating sound in the slur of the
    earth's blur.

The ineptitude of a clever man undirties thirty years of my shirt.
Perhaps a habit of music is not a bad thing.

The Great Defecator

Like the pooping peasant in Catalonia.
El Caganer, the great defecator, squats in this nativity scene or that.

John told me once that he'd tied his father to a tree, feeding him
 only castor oil and spit from a spoon his father kept tied to his
 left thumb.
I am not lying when I say that I sleep on my left side to protect my
 heart from all that people-hurt.

I saw myself write the same phrase three and one-third times, in
 each of four notebooks.
I keep it in an album of photographs of my now-dead dog.

There are secrets we tell no one.
Would you like to know how often I consider the weight of a certain
 woman's breasts?

Please don't tell anyone that my favorite color is green.
They only see me wrapped in burnt sushi leaves, in the rough
 brown language of trees.

Autumn. I had a hard time saying her fur and calling her *dead*.
Let me assure you: it is not *death* or *dog* or even *How can I possibly
 ever heal?*

Tonight it rained. Then it rained more. And now it keeps raining.
 Cats and.
It is as if part of me is leaking hormonally wrong, attacking this
 gland or that.

In conclusion, one or more of us is constantly releasing sorrow in all the wrong places.

To summarize, I plan to reread my friend Gene's *Dostoevsky and Other Nature Poems* and cry myself to sleep.

The Agony of Compassion

There was a need so sharp, even my pencil bled bloodless birds.
Ask for a hint, and speak eternal dice in the phrase, *agèd strange
   north.*

As if I was truly alive, I turned myself true, imagined the compass of
   an owl on fire in my chest.
A few excited crows rose like magnets, stirred decades-old
   buckshot above fall brush.

In those days, an ibis-colored weeping could be heard from thin
   river skin.
I don't know whether I'll ever be able to enjoy, again, the moon-
   lathed waves.

I tore each syllable apart from my mouth as if, for once, it didn't
   matter.
I recognized myself in the way wind said things over and through.

There was a blood-sore in my mouth—so real, my spine could
   enact.
I remembered blizzards, the quest for the South Pole. 1911 or '12.
   Eight Manchurian ponies slaughtered, compassionately, in the
   snow.

Colorblind

Or were they?
Does anything enjoy a healthy inadequacy among various levels of
　　music?

The signing of this tendency increases the desire to look back on
　　treaties of tonal demise.
I would demonstrate my mouth, through judo if necessary, if she
　　would but kiss it.

Ever since I missed the train to the stained-glass north, I have been
　　colorblind.
I liked perceiving continuity in the black ash of last year's smoke.

She became a complete human condition, even an enjoyable
　　history.
And before the seven meals were collected, we threw dice for my
　　bones.

Both waling, gray hairs sought a geometric bedpan in the waste
　　below the cut in a cholera cot.
I brushed up on algebra, on crochet, and prayed for the language of
　　the most south.

This is not a star-chart, she said, sinking her finger into the
　　quicksand of my chest.
It was then that I felt myself dissolve—breath by breath, tongue by
　　lip—into the moist of her mouth, the milk-crack slap of a
　　northbound track.

Each of Seven Months

Take care not to extract the carbon from my lower lip.
It is the best I can do with the Miró painting you scarred.

For a long time, the color of my fear was green. My grief, a warm
    saffron.
Once a month, I bit raw carrots, washed okra, and assumed every
    Japanese vegetable was medicinal.

I cut out the picture of the zebra you sent and made a collage.
I included the words *aching* and *habitual* at its jail-cell underbelly.

Sure, I revised the message on the answering machine.
Now it simply says, *Hello, we're not home, but here's the vulnerable*
    coat of the foal.

You say the magazine arrived from Bhutan, that you have beaten
    four of my poems for breakfast.
Careful, please, to heal their bruise. Burn them with kerosene,
    giving their ash to seven women—one on each day of the week,
    on the seventh month of the seventh year. Let them lie there,
    coal-fed and strong, on the tender tough of the tongue's torn.

The Difference Between Four and Five

Then the soup carriers arrived, each in leopard-skin robe.
My mouth was still stuck on a vowel, rich and exact, not unlike a
vermicular scraping.

Rilke spoke of the above equaling the below.
I was feeling vertical strength, even as I regarded the absent winter
worms.

Nothing tastes better in winter than French press decaf.
I lean into the press the way Leonard Bernstein jumped up on stage
and placed an ear to Charlie Haden's bass the first time Ornette
Coleman's quartet played the Five Spot.

The difference between the numbers four and five resembles the
midnight breathing of a contented dog.
Sure, I can cross any divide during music, or during a bluetick
hound's bay, as long as each note enters me while bringing the
entire universe with it.

Sometimes I want to keep a pet African tortoise and build it its own
room and love it for the duration of its ninety-year span.
I'm not talking about the metaphor of its shell, nor of the room, nor
any metaphor at all for that matter.

The Give Give Grief

What thick drench of speech arrives warm across our chest?
What little bit of spit?

There was the entwinement of tongues.
And I am left only with twos—left hand, right; hard mouth, soft; her
    desire, and the motion of moths.

Is it true that the danger of nitrogen narcosis means that
    compressed air cannot possibly be used at depths greater than
    thirty meters?
Whose lung is whose, and what in us both might burst due to our
    proximity to one another's mouths?

What I'm trying to say is that there are many depths.
What I mean is that I have died in what she holds privately moist
    and most shy.

I have been trying to breathe in at least one thousand and one
    ways.
Here, hold these ten centipedes together in your left hand while
    pouring the light of a kerosene torch through your right ear.

I have never been good at math.
I keep trying to multiply a louse and a flea, subtracting the cranes,
    all the while dividing my wingèd bleed into darker and most
    dark.

Little golden beak in the awful of my palm.
Let me stroke the quiet of your remarkable fright.

What drench of speech hides in the hollow of your bone?
My first word and last, the give give grieving of grief.

The Methodology of Rain

Settling my solid bones on the car's seat next to you resembles this:
a pearl caught in the throat of a wood thrush.
I am given, and I am whole. I return to you each of your floating
ribs.

When the doorbell had been alive inside our fear, I'd found a
pocket hanky of ants embroidered into the kitchen sink.
We'd answered to no one and let water swirls of coffee grounds
drag even our darkest selves down.

But did we crack open the locked door, let in the rain, fall through
one another's direction on our great migration north of south,
east of our lowest rib?
Might we just as easily have hit the road a day early and skipped
the tea, asking the waitress instead for a quarter or two for our
effort at her bitterest of smiles?

This weather is driving weather.
This bunch of bees' blood in my ear is a radio wave in a midnight-
dial-light-green blur.

Come to me, first, at arm's breath, then in every lengthening county
as jazz.
Come to me in Monk. In Blakey. In Cannonball Adderley. Break me
with Brahms. Let's discuss the day's suicide, excluding the
verbosity of talk-radio screech.

Devour me my ribs as your method. Your mouth-madness. Your
true.
Devour each of my ribs as your refuse and your rain.

The Deliberate Dead
of Continuously Laying Ourselves Bare

Something Private and Sly

Now we take up a rather complicated trick.
Travel the Copper River north and touch a coconut to your skull.

Expiate the Amazon and kill a walrus.
Fold yourself lengthwise through the White and Blue Nile at once,
    Upper Volta inconsolably below Lower Volta.

Sometimes I thirst for hunger. Other times, I taste everything I
    smell.
As to the large cow grieving milk to the raw of gray morning? I can
    only claim a crab claw in my mouth.

I cannot be held responsible for what you might say.
I have tried to coax you into digression, but a fever stint has
    shunted your mouth toward something inexplicitly sad.

We might sweat it out before we could even begin to bleed.
Leech ourselves silly and never experience the bombastic barium of
    an oyster's sudden release.

We might cocktail our soup, return strength through a straw.
We could and should and most definitely will, if only we might.

Some say I speak in Sutras to slowly lift the lid.
That I slit my, that I slowly cry, that I split my infinites into some
    definite private and sly.

Still, the exact weight of all things dead.
Still, a splice of mind laid out onto the tongue to wake beneath the
    lull of the dim, indispensable lamps.

The Incubation of *This* and *That*

We continue our examination of tangled autumn in my chest.
I receive you through the forest door of my breathing, through the
    ingenuity of all things dead.

If you are patient, wait here, nervously calming your joints.
Their inflammation of primordial remorse may shelter you with
    cacophonies of heat.

Together, the tiger cowry and muttonfish made extraordinary
    children.
My tongue was breeding a word up through you, tensing the arch in
    the sole of your foot.

Relax of it and accept. Tongue-twist my mouth. Refuse everything
    you refuse.
Hold me home. I might welcome your adorable hand as an
    afternoon of good long luck.

I thoroughly enjoyed your sympathy for the word *sympathy*.
Sorry, but you seemed to be saying you wanted the tiny red animals
    of our lie.

Yes, the fourth word of each sentence we break is always the
    phrase, *world without end*.
Probably the damp, heaped debris forty- or fifty-eggs deep.

The Indonesian turtle sank them into the amber-colored sand near
    a coral reef.
Everything was breath. Even my breathing blurred in and out of
    itself.

Uppermost in the incubation of *this* and *that* was a whole
   generation of shore birds actively seeking sorrow.
Many tons of original thought carried over as cracked shells.

There was vulnerability, and there was *vulnerability*.
My darling, we delved into the deliberate dead of continuously
   laying ourselves bare.

Invasive Species

It is a storm gully rocked hard with hail.
It is yesterday's match implanted in the hides of dread.

Herds of words, as if.
My *Oh, God*, my *ash gossip*, as if forced.

The life cycle of a water chestnut includes choking light out from
    the waiting throat of plankton.
The invasives from many words converge to converse me a bruise.

Nutria. Mute swan. Water beetle.
Water chestnut. Starling. Unfinished verb.

It is a storm but not a wind.
It is a rain but not the culinary kind.

It is a word choked at the root.
It is not so much but awfully hard.

Never does the eating orange nothing stunned from sky.
The buffalo blaze of the plains ignites a moment and then goes out.

The Momentary Anguish of Repair

The translucence of Upper Mongolia.
How I crave the slow bathwater of the moon.

We had been in search of a certain horse.
All summer it rained in the afternoon—periodically—like unbroken
  words *within* breaths and between them.

So it had been Montana and the Shields River Valley.
The buffalo jump outside my window expressed a most drastic
  descent.

The Cheyenne had a name for it—*This Roundness of Now.*
Fortunately, they did not speak its rough edge, nor wash away its
  salt.

Maybe we've simply come here to sit at a table and eat bread.
Maybe we've come, finally, in order to learn to bite something hard
  and die.

I am reconstituted daily in a patience of fur and a munching among
  shaggy hocks.
I keep a photo of a Mongolian pony, long dead. Her head bowed
  but not shaven.

Parsing of the Bowels

No, I rarely talk back to the plant that inhabits my stance.
It is there for a season I cannot decipher.

Some have called it summer. Others, the spring of autumn in a
    deutzia bush.
Others have relinquished every figure of salt at the parsing of the
    bowels.

I have expelled more of myself than I'd care to grow.
So many insecurities float in the bowl, like rhyming shreds of
    undigested love.

That's one reason I crave the naked solar plexus of a woman
    beneath my palm.
When the Indian sadhu placed his forefinger in my navel that
    evening in Banaras, even the dirt floor I lay on revolved.

We go round and round our own polar ice.
We search for passage safe as the hands of water, warmed in seal
    guts, freshly skilled.

We learn a craft. The reading of entrails. Struggle-clutch not to fall
    for this woman or that.
Not to develop new attachments just as we have come to relinquish
    the old.

We stand in showers, lie in tubs. We inhabit floors of thatched
    Banaras huts on hillsides, alone.
We tell ourselves we're getting clean but really want the skin to
    drop off. The insides of things to fall away. To burn apart.
    Dissolve.

More Than a Necessary Shedding

I am always waiting like the blind side of a coroner.
See, we are connected by more than cooperative floor joists.

Your monthly blood is more than a necessary shedding.
Believe me when I say I require your many moods to soothe me.

Beautiful sadness, how lovely your peace, your prerequisite of
    strain.
When I finally secure a position as a red fire ant I will expel the
    entire Gobi from within the grains of our mouths.

At that time, I will collect many sadnesses.
Others of my ilk might rely upon sugar cubes and breadcrumbs,
    upon a barrel of rainwater red with food coloring.

I am a sad judge, examining the radical implications of industrial
    labor.
In response to class war and gender inequity, I shout, *Enough!*
    Meaning, *A great exodus within one's blood is about to occur.*

The Powerful Dissolve of a Monk

It was a klaxon inscription of your tongue in mine.
We traveled to Guadalajara, incorporated the noise of cactus broth
    into our daily practice.

There are many fishes of vast color sequence.
The dream gave way to protocol and anticipated our indigenous
    demise.

It was short and only briefly painful.
It was much like trying to describe a dream of losing a baby tooth in
    a dream about the medical hazards of dreaming.

Let the orchestral fracture lightning-curve into jazz.
Place your lip bone on the tuning key of the sitar. Qualify as a
    substitute for the reconstitution of your favorite shade of green.

You let my daughter examine a freckle, a moss-pocked stone.
You knew I had no children, choked my bread-baking hand with
    austerities.

Coiled in the self-critical, in the heat, was the blood course of a boy
    and a vein that resembled a purposeful map.
I spider-slant the branch of the powerful dissolve of a monk.

We Louisiana-Purchase. We Lewis-and-Clark. We circumambulate
    cold feces in buffalo grass.
We seek to hollow one another out with the vast prairie slant of our
    tongue, a fierce dialect that mangles every third word into one.

You're Afraid of a Dead Echo?

I would be untruthful if I did not admit a blood-tinged complication.
The extreme limit of my mouth is a sound I have yet to bleed.

I feel it in my veins like a great bird scuffing the leech-clenched dirt.
I sense it in my sleep, even when I am perturbed with joy.

I shall torn-shed, and I shall weep.
I shall noun-splatter the most stringent intransitive ache.

Forever might I harp-seal an introverted syntax.
If inside my mouth, protected from the clubbing, then I might finally
    find.

What? you ask. *What* might I intravenously cough into you?
You're afraid of an unexplained dead echo replenishing itself in your
    brain?

Grand-Canyon this sad mule, then, as it takes one step on a dime.
See a penny; pick it up. All day long the mineral weeping of our
    birth will no longer be stuck.

There Are Many Beards in the Way One Sleeps

Arsenic was what we wanted, just by the sound of the word and the
    memory of Lorca's lobster.
Years before, I had been buried in Namibian sand up to my chest.

Thus protected, my heart could no longer ache, at least in public.
There are many beards, of course, in the way one sleeps.

At times like that, I am afraid of everything I speak.
Vertical or not, it is as if English has become the prolific waters of a
    clean-leaved tree.

Okay. We had to choose between speaking and being spoken.
At about three o'clock, the turnstone of a formidable exit flashed
    momentary green throughout the estuary.

Now I stayed the course of an individual word, leapt upon me in
    grains of *Please mark my nakedness*.
My emotions adopted an asexual method of reproduction common
    to the lower forms of life and death. Of living and breeding.
    Living and lying.

Critical Dispersal

I was born with a monkfish in each wrist.
Countless births blottered me with more *this*, less *that*.

I look at my Brahms CDs—the symphonies, concertos—and
    reconfigure a simple life.
Then I examine my hands and bear witness to sea-lice and eggs laid
    by the male seahorse.

At breakfast, César Vallejo and Alfonsina Storni take turns trying to
    impress me.
I never realized all the things you could do with blueberry compote
    and a shred of burnt toast on a pursed lip.

It they get it right, his mouth actually fits her papers.
If they get it right, the moon-scar on her rump has nothing to do
    with starlight sinning in the deaf man's ear.

Will you return to me everything she has said?
Will you tell me whether you ate meat together and what his worry
    resembled in the intimate dark?

We broiled the fish, ate it, and read the bones backwards and
    forwards at once.
More *this*, less *that*, somehow didn't matter—in her wind, in his
    voice—when we saw our large hands and mouths from inside
    one another's trembling molecule of salt.

Sorry

Now we return to sadness, to memory, to the dream of the three-
    ring binder piercing the dead possum at each pressure point.
We come to wearing shoes, to not wearing pants, to lying in a tub
    reading Bachelard, examining the intimate dark, soaking off the
    okra.

Pooled in primordial dissolution, I have been gifted a cambium
    tongue.
I lay it cautiously on your wrist. Imagine your red, red Sumerian lip.

Introducing food into the eye socket suggests a complex
    translation?
The body resists the past tense of every present verb, is nostalgic
    about things like words, participles perhaps, even heaviness in
    the letters *G* and *K*.

More specifically, I'm afraid sometimes of conflict and loss.
I remember growing up in a jar of Vicks VapoRub. The crush of
    croup and the gripping cough.

I remember thick blue pressure from all sides.
Squinting after the divorce when the sun stood over me with a sad
    shake of hair.

I remember features of the sky.
I remember wanting to grow up to be dust.

All this I'll name, *I'm sorry.*
Sorry for this, sorry for that. Sorry—even—to the possum for
    including it in the incessant rings of this unspeakable dream.

Extravagant Slaughter

Now I select the bladder of a sea turtle, green, accompanied by sun.
The sand itself drowses out the anus, remains of a blowfish stiffly
seeking refuge in the lower gears of the gut.

A very common species of language drops out of each of my words,
ranging from mottled gray to starling white.
Various shades of lies inhabit my phrase with great canopies of
sound.

Honestly, I don't think I've ever wanted a woman more.
That lifetime as a Torres Strait Islander vied for the most vulnerable
part of my heart, her scent hidden like a crowberry below my
tongue.

She required melancholy proof of the suspiration of my shy, even as
I touched alive my imagined touching of her.
Aspects of dugong grass were certainly harpoon-strong upon each
vantage point of what we shared across town as separate bouts
of sleep.

I honestly don't know which bone barb was attached to the coil of
my throated thought.
I'd say things and then only later would they manifest as soiled
proof.

That boil on the yogi's arm was brought on only by a line of mind.
The dedicated lance drained away all doubt and sway into the
cosmogonic egg.

Dear one, that mole on your left breast.
I glimpsed a spark of the darkest light of my life that I could live
inside and thrive.

There is a primitive yet efficient impulse of inhabiting our most
intimate dark.
I fell into a simple description of extravagant slaughter, the plentiful
length and shy of my eye.

Trying to Track Down Your Least-Open,
Your Cracking-Closed, Heart

Which brings me to the word *gurry*.
Which brings me to the definition *fish offal*.

Origin unknown, I was beside myself with guinea fowl as if it were
    me with the black plumage and small white spots.
Through no fault of my own, I had—almost unobtrusively—become
    domesticated in the hen yards of Africa.

There was the closed door of an ovary.
An egg was cracking open on its own sadness.

The bowl is not round nor clear nor sitting plaintively by an open
    sea.
See the bird perched on the windowsill, pecking its own reflection?

Kites, you say, as if we both feared the lightning and the flight. As if
    somewhere, present tense was past.
But tell me, which of us inverted the sky by tying the tail? Which,
    the earth upon which we plead?

Everything I Have Ever Sad
Somehow Says Through You

In All My Blindness

All my poetry *compañeros*, like avuncular stew, stir my late-night
  dead.
Vallejo. Hernández. George Seferis. Even Takahashi soup.

When we interrupt ourselves, introduce a splinter of Japanese or
  Greek, where do we find the termite-induced wood?
I am busy translating myself into dissolve, into one of the three lost
  languages of salt.

I have written about being born many times as no one else's
  duplicate.
Carbon copy the carbon data of my wrist. Keep at least a ring of
  smoke for yourself.

When I went to the funeral home for my friend I imagined my own
  last song.
Would it be Ravi's *Raga Bhimpalasi*? Jimi's underwater guitar?
  Yogananda's chants? Or, simply, afternoon roof-scratch of a
  displaced possum or raccoon?

What do we hear when we step, finally, to and from the nocturnal
  mud?
When they gather to admire the mortician and honor a wrist
  well-bled?

Last week, I watched a film about baby leopards and warthogs.
I imagined sloshing in my own warthog hole, climbing over my
  littermates, pleading (in all my blindness) to the lush African
  night for the necessary touch of the ponderous—filthy—teat.

The Journey Inward (Body Time No More)

From that which refuses my moth, I replace my hands.
From that which instigates the winter storms of my eyes, I open
    an ear.

On the pillow, a spot of snail blood, spittle of the vanished auk.
Where my left ear had lain in the moist warm, all noise of the world
    was muffled.

Draw a bath of lightly caressed playing cards.
Ask me for the king of clubs, the jack of night sweats.

There is a place in my heart even I have not touched with
    diamonds.
Try if you must, but know that—in extreme quiet—you too might
    get quashed.

A divide opens up along the shelf of Antarctic ice.
On one side of the deck, it is cold. On the other, cold.

I do not speak any longer in ice moths or in irreparable twos.
I will not solve the dichotomy of this wingèd pain, even with an
    obstinate mouth.

Nor will I salve my own blue-bolstered bruise with dream talk and
    shame.
I am not talking body time any longer but a continental drift of ice
    diamonds, devoid of the clutch of a kind hand or mouth.

Of Course

Where is my aggression if not inside the flake of red pepper?
If you removed my hands, what color would your mouth be?

I kept a pet mouse named *Indian Braided Rug*.
All I'd have to do was call him *Henry*, and he'd ignore me.

The burners of the gas range are excellent mouse tunnels.
I have come to the end of my weakness and am strange.

Give me a cigarette, sexily crushed with your stiletto heel.
Smoke it for me afterwards, or caress my thoughts while we lie
    listening to the couple in the next room begin to massage fruit
    and vegetables for dinner through the thin pleading of the wall.

I know you might not want to discuss the profit of selling a finger.
Point the way. Of course, I will find the bathroom and flush twice.

If I Were the Direction West

I'm always collecting words.
Once, when I was alive, I found the word *dread*, splintered, there, in
a stick inside my right cheek.

For sixty-two years I have borne the body armor of a gnat.
I have been as slow-moving as any possible blight.

Around the settlement were huge qualities of salt.
The grave of a German explorer in Bushrata entranced me.

How could the eye so blind?
How could I know then what I've only now described?

And so I collected the word *ivory*. I collected *gorgeous* and *buxom*.
I ensconced the phrase, *Invigorate my words with a bit more saliva.*

If I were the direction west, how would you know whether my
moon had bruised, whether my tobacco was finally acceptable?
If I called myself *Fairly Safe*, why wait for me at the depot fully
closed? Why redden your mouth with the stinging juice of a
beet?

A Pattern of Dexterity

As to the dark red groan of oolong tea, I relinquish all thirst.
I even hand you back your stockings, choosing, instead, to sniff a
    fishnet of ground nutmeg.

Sometimes it's a long day, alone, without mussing myself.
Sometimes it's a life and a half before we kiss the marble floor that
    touched so many foreheads in the temple.

I am not speaking of a pattern of dexterity.
That would surely leave a hole in my how and why.

I am not talking of *not* talking.
That is to open the door thirteen times without encumbrance.

If you love me, improve it, like a crow might restate a pasture.
Improve it, like a woman who walks into a room.

The expiration date of the sycamore leaves is stamped in the
    ossicles of my inner ear, stapled to the little sound in my lung.
Open the door, turn left, and hand me a false épilobe, the medicinal
    plant we might eat to suffer the scrofula's release.

Mournful in Open Country

Had given myself a bone.
Had placed it slantwise into my wrist.

You could come to me as if you were a scale insect in search of
    honey, attaching yourself and collecting—then secreting—the
    fluid.
You could say even *that's* still sweet, that we should cherish what
    we pass.

My past? Why have I ripped open the heart of a green pepper every
    day this month looking for a dead goldfinch?
A sybaritic feast? An excretion of noisy rock sparrows confiscating
    my ear?

The cliché says to get on with it, to release the goldfinch of groaning
    old, to bury the dread.
I have never believed in clichés. I believe the hunting call of the
    hyena, mournful in open country.

Had given myself. Had placed a. Had *could-come-to-me-as-you-wish*
    and *secretion of salt.*
An excavation of noise is still sweet as the insect part of my heart
    secreting honey—stings and all—into a round, flat cake, sweet in
    taste, tender even to the tongues of monks.

The Exact Cost of Fish

Shared bread brings the cost of food down outside the purview of
my knee.
In the cage, footsteps come toward my own poise of thunder.

The lightning adjourned to three-quarter time, that is, to pacing-
panther time.
A list of all my neckties was written with the blackest disappearing
ink.

We hung the polished shoes out to dry with the sheets.
The Venetian blinds gave the room even slats of sunlight that
embroidered the floor.

Some evenings we had to cope with a lifetime of strict animal debt.
We built a sort of street, perhaps a canal of bones, full of Surrealist
photographs in which the collage actually improved our features.

Do I want to eat the penny or place it threateningly inside the
peony blossom?
Can I complete my plush social studies in a timely manner that
includes the hidden classicism of the working class?

Throw the big cat the exact cost of fish to match her even pacing, all
evening, back and forth as if a riverous blood.
I don't understand zoos or economics or the filthiest coffin of an
exhausting history. The suddenness of a feline waul.

Everything I Have Ever Sad Somehow Says Through You

You may speak by name, speak by my very, yet leave out the nouns.
Words like *sadness*, *stream*, or *(young-man's) dance* constitute me
the syntactic slip of too much breeze.

I eat a floppy crayfish. I inscribe, slantwise into your heart, its stool.
Everything I have ever sad somehow says through you.

In 1961, there were only thirty-six whooping cranes left in the
world.
How this figure shaped me. How it childhood and fear. How it stuck
in my mouth like soap.

Here, take the x-ray of my lower lip and study the multiple cause of
shame.
Fracture the silence with a kiss. Plural me into your tongue.

I am slow to tongue your mouth and mix the seed.
What of our shared vocabulary will you wash down with juice?
Which will you kiss back into me when I find your mouth with
words like *Cole River* or *star-shaped track*?

There is nothing more beautiful than caressing the cranes as they
river-dance my disease.
I will not touch them, nor wish upon their strut, nor force my mouth
upon their vulnerable throat, for fear of invigorating their loss.

Let them fly. Let them sand-lice. Let them egg-lay without a crack.
Do not bring them to our bed. I want their numbers to improve.

Proof of the Theorem of Rising Hills

Daily, it is not my nose that bleeds.
Cauterize my memory of Greek avgolemono soup. The sensual
　　cricket may never betray you.

You seem perfectly content to roast green peppers but eat the
　　yellow ones raw.
You appear to have a fondness for furnace talk—the congestive
　　highs and lows of the day.

If you want proof of the theorem of rising hills, measure the
　　regularity of my breath.
If you require the discovery of a dime in each ear, replenish the
　　magician with hidden doves.

I have been either an empty monastery or an eight-hundred-year-
　　old house.
Ioanna wrote from a marsh and, from across that brackish water,
　　sent me her trembling of sea mice.

Now I doubt the sorcerer eats all three halves of the orange.
It's Moroccan and contains four Arabian horses and glass fragments
　　of sound.

This was either a complicated start to tomorrow or a simple ending
　　to today.
I've made at least three attempts at being friendly. Help me to cut
　　my loss.

Two Women Whose Clear Heads Cut Clear Through to Sad

They were kissing not the lips but the secret the other's head held.
These two women cradled life more than the dead teak from which
    they were carved.

A document burning in the head of a librarian. In Paris. In Prague. In
    the African bush.
She is dying of some disease known only as *We Slept the Animal*.

A burnt starfish in the chest is the very pulsing of a flower as it dies?
A saddle stitch in a book of poems suppresses all that wants to fly
    off the page?

Twinspur diascia. These women were the three sides of a coin.
Some part of us mirrored back as neither *this* nor *that*.

These women were elm-burn, Saturn-turn, bushwillow in the
    horizontal scar of a star.
They were two men inside themselves, dying as if the boy-child was
    a grown girl.

Honestly, my tongue hurt just saying such things.
Your tongue too, as it strained to speak the sleep salts carved
    whole.

They were kissing. Years, minutes. The aches of maraca-shake the
    head held.
Kissing life clear out of the wood, as we do each day just in the
    great goodbye of hello.

The head was a basket was a fishbowl a womb was the shape of all
things dear and dead and dearly dead.

Catalogs of peace broke water in the brain, unwept books burning
the librarian from inside *in*. *Gold carp in the throat*, she repeated.
Gold carp in the throat.

Ravens Dirging My Chest

Yes, you are my mask. I wear my conception of you frown to frown.
No, I did not take your raisins, nor eye your shoelaces with lust.

There is a fierce squabbling of ravens dirging my chest.
I feel the long needle of their beak interrogate my ribs.

Such distance in describing pain is not new.
I wear my contraption of you ghost-mouth to ghost-mouth.

They say we are always looking through the lens of death.
They explain that this will measure the wolf content of our DNA.

I understand you will clarify the butter prior to ingesting the snails.
The entire sky of Brahmanical soot will unfold as smoke-tree slosh
    and ill-conceived ash.

Slowly, you will see cloud-cover as song. Will believe me and make
    me your mouth.
You will regard your relationship with a shoelace as cleansingly
    clean. As pleasantly platonic. As honorably sad.

The Cause and Effect of Multiple Births

Emblems of *don't-know* or *maybe-should* translate the terrace of
    my nose.
I am not fond of color. I am beautiful as a palm frond on fire.

You ask about the bok choy, whether I soaked the leaves and
    simmered them in paprika.
It gives us strength, like a street sign telling every intersection in
    two names.

I can't say for sure whether I am a casual acquaintance at the
    corner of *Here* and *Nothingness*.
I suppose it depends upon whether you ask the neighbor or the
    flake of dried parsley in my tea.

With workers aloof and exhausted, we witness the construction of a
    thirteenth-floor tree house.
The long neck of *this-then*, of the brightest and the hinge, might
    swing me back into the volatility of pants.

I've worn my hair long as long as I can recall. It may have to do with
    my many former lives on the banks of the Ganges.
There are conditional vowels, scrolled across the pillow each
    morning, giving me answers to the cause and effect of my
    multiple births. The way my breathing blurs me back, time and
    again, into this breathing, perfectly slurred.

River Crossing

They made the river crossing in spring—life after life—and it was
    daringly dangerous.
Some bore horses, oxen, crates of pears, even—unknowingly—jars
    of avian flu.

While I might objectify the opportunity of chance, you tell me the
    world is nothing but drift.
I recognize my obsessive self in the spit-shine of your shoe.

Three months from now I may tire of boredom.
I might hand-saw your thought, kiss an invisible tree growing from
    the navel of this woman or that.

That's impossible, you say. *No one can inhabit the internal lamps of*
    another.
Just ask Delvaux. Just creep along his spine like feminine spider
    moss craving moon-feed.

We marvel at the way the fox sniffs the ice and does not wet its tail.
We comprehend why we are always giving ourselves over to birth.

Mud Cells of Excellent Milk

The Sad Textile of Your Eye

Back in the paddock, my Tunis sheep were shy.
Even my spacious geography could not account for a few ewes in
    labor.

Simple fragment of double-weave plain cloth.
Blue is more prominent than green in the sad textile of your eye.

To steady my courage, I asked for your hand in hatred.
We were quite a pair, standing that way shoulder to shoulder,
    daylight mercilessly revealing our scar.

I loved the paintings attributed to our body parts.
My chest hair had apparently drawn a pair of six-fold screens from
    the Muromachi period in Japan.

We open the jar of cashew butter, consider how many lives we
    have eaten just to arrive, here, at this kitchen counter?
We consider Bunsei, that he appears to be a follower of the Zen
    artist-monk, Shūbun, but that details of his life remain sketchy.

When the night is incredibly still, the animals, in all their nocturnal
    dead, remain quiet.
Each one echoes the sound of an irregular rasping of a hermit crab
    surfacing from an unoccupied burrow.

Shall we exchange breaths from deep within our mutual solitude?
Shall I deposit the angioplasty of my sperm into the corrosive
    thread of your egg?

That Moment of Wept

What I know is a kind of brief reflex.
What I know is an enactment of leopard blood, sunspots shot
   across the dark hour.

I realize that the waves hold my broken, that the other end of
   thunder is a sad disposition.
That the notebook's spiral that connects each page reminds me of
   the introduction of salt into each of the three lower ribs.

You confiscate my mouth, try to force my singing sideways so the
   pain won't slip.
You say your heart is protected, that you enjoy having it live in a
   cage, that feeling *anything* is good, even if only the wrong side of
   a coin.

When the Cossacks danced their brotherly let-me-kiss-you dance,
   one by one they told us what we had most feared.
This loneliness. *That* moment of wept.

I am done with vodka slosh, done with tricking myself into a Russian
   Orthodox spire, with caring for a kind confessional cast as a
   coffee klatch or exhausted rain.
I hunt the umbrella head of mushrooms and find the exclusionary
   oil that might take me to intimate foreign places inside where I
   suddenly become an adept conversationalist.

Reversing the Gaze

I do not recall the salt extracts you expired.
I read that you have reversed the gaze of every appropriated
    culture you have ever bled.

I have carried over my weeping as a lost paragraph.
I open it in public, insert a word, but it refuses to say anything
    clean.

Do not ask me to interrogate the Bengali cricket.
It has lodged in my throat, and I am working toward its release.

The spread of tuberculosis is difficult, if not impossible, to track.
Something is restless in the decaying peacock they have sewn
    slantwise into my chest.

And if I return your forms, if you recall the notary, will she examine
    the cut lotus?
I'm sure no one else is even close to detecting its scriptural tease.

The abundance of forts in Rajasthan is painful to discern. More
    painful to enact.
I have been stripping layer after layer of red sandstone from my
    spine—not like the thin of an onion but in the thick tradition of
    boiling the blubber of a long-sought whale.

The One I Named

That year the seal hunt proved overly unproductive.
I had left Kwangchow two lifetimes back, somehow crossed the
    Bering Strait without a footbridge, coming into the womb of
    another possibility.

Let's arrange a few moist phrases to see what we have.
Let's start with *flensing the seal skin*, with *the yelping of excited
    dogs*, with *a menstruating woman on the birthing rug is said to
    be dangerous to a child about to be born*.

Look at the stars and count your life backwards into nothing but
    repair.
Black, white. Black, white. Black, white, white, white.

I know. There is short notice of a told apotheosis in my expected.
The figure eight of my heart is not a giant epoxy-resin statue of
    Mao.

Such tongue bumps gave me pause.
It was not typhus, at least not typhus of any tongue I grew.

I cleared my throat, built a neighborhood entirely of caribou skin
    and snow.
I looked at my star—marked on my forehead all the way from the
    womb—felt its kinship pull calling out to me, *The one who
    named me, the one I named*.

Mud Cells of Excellent Milk

I will have traveled backwards through the rejoicing of entrails of a
    dead hippopotamus.
I must absolutely stop body waxing the oatmeal schmear across my
    chest.

If a meager fire offered a contrary cough, how might the clumsy
    hair-strength of camp light become rude?
If I respelled Sheila's name as *Shelagh*, would she attach her search
    for impatience to my curious code of boiled pigeon eggs?

I found one—one life—in a nest of plump dead grass outside
    Brazzaville.
I ate the grass, and the mud cells of excellent milk expanded my
    chest as mason bees built a wall of hungry flight.

She took lipstick and wrote in her diary, *Shall I capitalize "African
    Goliath Beetle" so as to make it appear even larger?*
She was always very careful when it came to removing bamboo
    splinters, sensuously, from my spleen.

At the going away party, we listened, in a circle, to songs of the
    Siberian shaman and danced to sixties Motown music, to ice
    commingling with worm castings in the eaves.
My friend was headed to Botswana. I returned home to read Gide's
    journals from the twenties on the Congo, reveled in his critique
    of colonialism, and beheld extreme flecks of buckshot even in
    the sparrows picking strangely fathered grain from the cruel salt
    flats of what we took to be Indiana snow.

African Sleep Sickness

I cannot say whether I trekked from Bambane to Ujiji in quest of the
    Nile, or even in search of some form of *Am I good enough?*
What I know is there was a river, a seventy-three-days march, and
    ulcers on my feet beneath an enormous canopy of screw palms.

Show me the tree under which they buried the heart and viscera.
Show me a kind talk of falls, the way water struggles against an
    enormous rainbow.

This was not two years of advanced human remains.
This was the Zambezi Valley. Lake Dilolo. And everywhere, tsetse
    flies bit the underbelly of an ox.

Were these our words? Unresolved sexual fantasies surfacing now
    as the sleep sickness?
Were we aching into ourselves—not in the comforting love-grasp
    but with having never quite grown up?

Or were they words of the well-sung? We had been known to trek
    through ooze—coarse bamboo, splinters in the wet, and a
    coughing black mud.
Someone brought a rhinoceros egg. Said the dream was from
    centuries before.

The Hindu scriptures say it takes more than a million lives *just to
    become human.*
Red driver ants abled my observations into a quite featureless
    spring.

Wet, wet memory of childhood habit-stanced my glance.
Years later, I even read that for five coils of copper I milked maggots
    for twenty minutes from my toes.

If you make me porridge with sour goat milk, I might remember my
    many mothers.
Here, touch this finger. Tell me which of my past lives upon which
    you most thrived.

Border of Yes, Contusion of No

Yes, my childhurt hurt.
But whose did not? What birth—even hatching from the egg—is
    not a fierce form of mending?

Mist of inmost regret.
I regret that I have not regretted you enough.

There is an unanswered letter on my desk.
It is either *Y* or *N*, or perhaps some yet-to-be-discovered vowel on
    which I have based my life.

The people with sun-kissed hair had many years of the very dark.
Nothing is truer than paradox. We often move through the world—
    as if it *were* the world—with the fanning brilliance of a peacock's
    plaintive plea.

The Sacred and the Profane

There must be a prize for counting to three hundred?
Three hundred breaths. Three hundred days into the year. Blood
   pheasants, say, stored in the gut. A three-hundredth Sutra.

She willingly owled my regret with calculated hunger.
Will you permit me to redress your wounds with night thunder?

I sense your memory of saliva searching the complicated caves of
   body salts.
There is a sensation of candlesticks in my hand, as if someone said
   chakra, then *seven churches*, and, finally, *seven holy lamps in the
   spine*.

This tremendous angel of how I might regret.
I am incapable of reptile service, even if I exude a warm green as
   the common commission of my ear.

I don't want to be allowed to count backwards by threes—or even
   by the hundreds—while you elongate your ankle to flatter the
   shaving cut on your leg.
Let me touch the length of desire you relinquish, with each floating
   rib, into the bathwater accepting your dirt as its own. Accepting
   my dirt as belonging to you. As belonging to what of you I most
   want to become.

The Texture of Milk

You insist that I embrace each Sutra in multiple positions.
I prevent your mouth. I ask your mask.

It was dusk in my mouth and in the susceptible bone of the throat.
A Galápagos finch swallowed a worm two-and-two-thirds-centuries
    deep.

It is not enough to endear myself to each mole on your neck.
I have understood too well the texture of blending milk and ash, fire
    and the skilled bruise of your skin.

Still, I return time and again to considering the extinct exoskeleton
    of a Gobi rat.
Some desert heat from below tells me it—and *only* it—will be the
    only thing that feeds.

If We Could Practice Each Other, We'd Be the World

Her glowed hand when she hungry-shaped his shoulder.
His thank-you-for-touching-me when she declared him alive.

Her insensate will to live, as if a singular freedom and a truly
    handsome format.
His sweat-covered skin, as if it carried over from cat-scratch lives.

So the butterfly contained in the body does not cry out?
So the body is a cage, and we are caught by bones of sleep as we
    wind-current our dissolve into the impossible bodies of birds?

Come where I can most see you.
Let me have full view of your meditation and its ease.

Mounds of space between breaths leave us in the sensuous cold of
    cemetery madness.
If we could practice each other, we'd be the world.

Well Short

Well short of complete emotional maturity, I pick a scab.
Its soft brown blood is a tired god whose gratings fall in shavings to
cover my awful and my hurt.

Sure, I have bathed several times a week these past years,
searching for a way to soften my lives.
Yes, my mother was a Pisces, as was her mother, and even my
father's, and now it appears I have Pisces ascendant in my
stream.

So it turns out the circle of lightning is not a circle at all? That I have
lived not in the estuary of an eel in heat but in an enlivening
swamp?
It turns out the jagged branch continuously reaching toward me is
electric beyond repair?

When mosquitoes bite the bottom of my heart, I know the moon
has returned.
When the dreams of Zulu and Umbete rake their coals unknowingly
through my night sweats, it appears we've all been massacred in
slaughtering—just in thought—a command of legionary ants.

This frightening blood-broom is something to pick at, to blur.
Mute falling away of road dust. The owl clocking its neck, shaking
off my rage. A swan measuring my one good breath, circling the
pond again and again.

Almost Imaginable

Often, the most condemned authorization is adult.
This does not mean that time is distinct—only a sorry recital of
    rectitude.

We gamble enthusiastically on an illegal butterfly fight.
You are not on the take but express a host of nervous humiliation
    when both bugs die, in a rough part of town, disguised as our
    body parts.

If my mouth was boarded shut. If the window splint. If I woke with a
    moth in my chest, would you touch my cheek as if you and the
    moth were married?
If you weren't married to it, would you place your tongue in my ear
    as if the bee resin made us both partially alive?

Please forgive my slantwise grasp of pain.
I keep asking forgiveness from everyone—every *wing*—asking
    others to teach me to forgive myself for everything I might have
    done. Everything almost imaginable.

Curious

Curious how the rest of my life is a Paiute encampment, how my
    mind bends wind back through the Pawnee Grasslands.
The body of emotional poverty this time around was a small glad
    glance.

Had I not nursed a glass of seltzer water, I would most certainly not
    have heard the swallowing of stars.
If you count my charred ribs, ask which of us rode off victorious—
    they will total the minutes of scar-scraped sleep.

Alright. I struggle to make sense of how my mouth invigorates your
    most hidden.
I am employed by your bamboo cane, your faint of it and *ah* and
    oh-so-tensing muscular fade.

Let me lean on every passion-word you have ever translated from
    the Chinese.
Let me geisha-straw, let me Japan, let me full milk of your mouth.

Come to me as you come down and up and through the bodiless
    breathing of plants.
Come to me without moving, like a furnace grate confounded by
    flowers.

Curious how not just the Pawnee—but the Mongols, the Vikings,
    the Shōguns, the Greeks—gave me a spear slit in the dark that
    resembled our later commingling of years.
Curious how your peacock and my phoenix. How I one day and this
    cut. How I just might. How in some life or other, finally arrive.

Notes

The epigraphs are from George Stanley, *Flowers*, White Rabbit Press, 1965, and from Takiguchi Shūzō, translated by Miryam Sas and quoted in her *Fault Lines: Cultural Memory and Japanese Surrealism*, Stanford University Press, 1999.

The closing words in the title of "Nothing Is Ever as Clearly Written as the Owl's Insomnia" pay homage to the title of Rafael Alberti's *The Owl's Insomnia*, selected and translated by Mark Strand, Atheneum, 1973.

In "Cut," the concept that taking on a new body in a fresh incarnation "is like putting on an old overcoat," is a paraphrase of a statement often repeated by Paramahansa Yogananda, in lectures and books, to describe the restrictiveness of the human form.

"The Great Defecator" is for John Bradley, who sent me a news article about this strange and marvelous character, *El Caganer*.

"Invasive Species" is dedicated to Annie Chappell.

"Two Women Whose Clear Heads Cut Clear Through to Sad" was written in response to a teakwood and iron sculpture, "Mind's Cage," by Indian artist, Karl Antao, and accompanied a reproduction of this artwork in *International Gallerie: A Journal of Ideas* (Mumbai, India), Volume 13, Number 2, 2010.

In "River Crossing," for the phrase, "*the internal lamps of another*," see note in "The Sacred and the Profane," immediately below.

"The Sacred and the Profane" takes its title from Mircea Eliade's *The Sacred and the Profane: The Nature of Religion*, Harcourt Brace Jovanovich, 1956. The phrase, "*seven holy lamps in the spine*," transforms the Hindu-yogic concept of the light of each chakra, at the same time borrowing and building upon Virginia Woolf's phrase, "The lamp in the spine," in *A Room of One's Own*, Harcourt Brace & Company, 1991.

More poetry published by SurVision Books

Noelle Kocot. *Humanity*
 (New Poetics: USA)
 ISBN 978-1-9995903-0-7

Ciaran O'Driscoll. *The Speaking Trees*
 (New Poetics: Ireland)
 ISBN 978-1-9995903-1-4

Elin O'Hara Slavick. *Cameramouth*
 (New Poetics: USA)
 ISBN 978-1-9995903-4-5

Anatoly Kudryavitsky. *Stowaway*
 (New Poetics: Ireland)
 ISBN 978-1-9995903-2-1

Christopher Prewitt. *Paradise Hammer*
 (Winner of James Tate Poetry Prize 2018)
 ISBN 978-1-9995903-9-0

Anton Yakovlev. *Chronos Dines Alone*
 (Winner of James Tate Poetry Prize 2018)
 ISBN 978-1-912963-01-0

Bob Lucky. *Conversation Starters in the Language No One Speaks*
 (Winner of James Tate Poetry Prize 2018)
 ISBN 978-1-912963-00-3

Maria Grazia Calandrone. *Fossils*
  Translated from Italian
  (New Poetics: Italy)
  ISBN 978-1-9995903-6-9

Sergey Biryukov. *Transformations*
  Translated from Russian
  (New Poetics: Russia)
  ISBN 978-1-9995903-5-2

Anton G. Leitner. *Selected Poems 1981–2015*
  Translated from German
  ISBN 978-1-9995903-8-3

Our books are available to order via
http://survisionmagazine.com/books.htm